The Delaplaine
2020 Long Weekend Guide

Andrew Delaplaine

GET 3 FREE NOVELS
Like political thrillers?
See next page to download 3 FREE page-turning
novels—no strings attached.

**NO BUSINESS HAS PAID A SINGLE PENNY OR GIVEN
ANYTHING TO BE INCLUDED IN THIS BOOK.**

Senior Editors - *Renee & Sophie Delaplaine*
Senior Writer - **James Cubby**

Gramercy Park Press
New York London Paris

WANT 3 *FREE* THRILLERS?

Why, of course you do!

If you like these writers--
Vince Flynn, Brad Thor, Tom Clancy, James Patterson,
David Baldacci, John Grisham, Brad Meltzer, Daniel
Silva, Don DeLillo
If you like these TV series –
House of Cards, Scandal, West Wing, The Good Wife,
Madam Secretary, Designated Survivor
You'll love the **unputdownable** series about
Jack Houston St. Clair, with political intrigue, romance,
suspense.

Besides writing travel books, I've written political thrillers for
many years that have delighted hundreds of thousands of
readers. I want to introduce you to my work!
Send me an email and I'll send you a link where you can
download the first 3 books in my bestselling series, absolutely
FREE.

Mention **this book** when you email me.

andrewdelaplaine@mac.com

DID YOU FIND AN INTERESTING PLACE?
If you discover a place you think I should check out on my next visit, drop me a line, will you? I'll mention your name if I end up listing it.
andrewdelaplaine@mac.com

MEXICO CITY
The Delaplaine
Long Weekend Guide

TABLE OF CONTENTS

Chapter 1
WHY MEXICO CITY?

I love Mexico City, even though the first time I
traveled there, with my mother, we almost brought
her back in a box. She had made the mistake of using
the ice cubes in her hotel room fridge to make a drink
instead of pouring bottled water into the ice trays.

Boom!

You're sick as a dog.

But that was many years ago. Generally, I've had
nothing but wonderful times in Mexico City.

When I think about what Mexico City was and how it came to be what it is today, my mind still boggles.

You have to remember that the whole city is built on a drained lake bed. When there was still a lake, around 1325, it was established as the Aztec capital called Tenochititlán. The island in the middle of the lake was reached by way of a series of causeways. This was what Hernan Cortes found when he showed up in 1521. He promptly destroyed it.

Mexico has a rich and bloody history, not unlike all the other countries in the New World where the indigenous populations where slaughtered or enslaved. (But one has to remember that Cortes didn't do anything to the Aztecs that the English settlers didn't do to the Indians.)

The altitude is high, over 7,000 feet, so if you come from a low-lying coastal area, be prepared for some difficulty in breathing. And while the government has made enormous strides in cleaning up the famously polluted air in Mexico City, it's still pretty awful. You have to pray for good air. But you can never be sure of it.

There are things about Mexico in general that you want to be aware of if you want to travel wisely—and safely. The State Department says 14 of the 31 states (and Federal District, or *Distrito Federal*, or D.F., which is Mexico City) have no travel warnings. The others you want to avoid because of the drug-related gang warfare that's an ongoing reality in Mexico, responsible for ripping the country apart. (Americans are really to blame, since we're the ones buying all the drugs.)

One of the reasons Mexico City is so much more safe than other parts of the country is that everybody wants to be able to come here and visit it in peace, and this includes a lot of the high-end drug dealers, many of whom have houses and families here. They don't want to come here and duel it out on the streets the way they do elsewhere.

Of the 20 top foreign locations for Americans, 4 are in Mexico: No. 2 is Cancun, followed by No. 3, Playa del Carmen, Cabo san Lucas / Los Cabos at No. 11 and Puerto Vallarta at No. 15.

One good thing about Mexico City is that it has been sidestepped by the drug cartels so there's no sense of the overwhelming violence that occurs in other parts of Mexico.

You will find the *Distrito Federal* (Federal District, another name for the city) to be quite a beautiful, handsomely laid-out city.

Lay of the Land

At 571 square miles, D.F.—as Mexico City residents, or *chilangos*, call it—is vast, but visitors gravitate to a few key neighborhoods.

Centro Histórico: Anchored by the Zócalo plaza, the historic center is a mix of monuments and bustling commerce.

Roma: Hipsters, artists, and boutique owners have revived this once-bourgeois neighborhood of Art Nouveau mansions.

Condesa: In Mexico City's answer to New York's West Village, shops, restaurants, and apartments radiate out from the Parque México.

Polanco: One of the city's poshest districts keeps expanding north: "Nuevo Polanco" is being colonized by galleries and shopping malls.

Getting Around Safely: Taxis are plentiful, but you may feel more secure having a private car. From Journey Mexico at www.journeymexico.com

For the latest safety information, go to the U.S. State Department at travel.state.gov.

CASH & DEBIT CARDS.

Notify the companies whose cards you use that you are going to Mexico. Transactions might be blocked if you don't. Have them send you alerts or call you if any charge looks suspicious. When using ATMs, try to avoid street side ATMs in favor of ATMS inside a bank or other business.

Have credit card numbers and other information written down in a safe place.

You'll need cash because a lot of places don't accept plastic. But get your currency converted before going to Mexico because you'll stick out as a foreigner by getting it done at the airport when you land. (The rates are high there too.) A lot of currency exchange booths are not in secure areas, so beware.

YOUR DRESS.

You're not in Vegas, you're in a potentially dangerous city, so leave the shorts and flip-flops at home unless you're visiting the beach somewhere. Don't be an obvious tourist. Keep your camera in your travel bag, not around your neck.

YOUR PHONE.

Don't be glued to it the way so many people are, not when you're out on the streets. You're begging for trouble.

Check with your carrier to find out what the fees are when traveling in Mexico.

Chapter 2
GETTING ABOUT

UBER
https://www.uber.com/global/en/cities/mexico-city/

Helpful tips from Uber

There's an extensive Metro system, a bus system, a trolley system. I would avoid them all unless you *really* know your way around. I never use them. Never.

They even have special cars on the Metro system for women only because women get groped on the mixed cars. Also there's the constant threat of pickpockets. Stay away.

Mexico City is one of the world's largest cities and boasts an estimated population of 21 million people living in the region. Mexico City is divided into 16 areas known as delegaciones, not unlike New York's boroughs. These areas are further divided into neighborhoods called "colonias" and there are about 250 of these.

When traveling the city, it is important to know which colonia that you're traveling to and be aware that some have duplicate or very similar names. Visitors to Mexico City need to take note of the increase in crime and safety concerns that are prevalent in the city.

While traveling throughout Mexico City by public transportation can be economical, it is not always the safest mode of transportation and warnings regarding use of public transportation should be respected.

Locals and those familiar with Mexico City travel freely and cheaply via the Metro, first- and second-class buses.

However, visitors should travel by ***sitio taxis*** (official taxis registered to a specific locale or hotel), as these taxis are fairly inexpensive and the safest means of travel within the city.

"Turismo" and Sitio Taxis

These two methods are the safest means of travel within Mexico City. Turismo taxis, un-marked cabs, are usually luxury cars that are assigned to specific hotels and are identified by their special license plates. These may be more expensive that other taxis but they are the safest.

Established rates are fixed for travel to and from the airport. However, rates for traveling to other destinations and sightseeing need to be negotiated with the drivers.

The bell captain at your hotel can tell you what the airport fare should be and make sure to confirm with the cab driver before departure. Theses cab drivers, usually licensed English-speaking guides, can be excellent tour guides and provide valuable information regarding Mexico City.

While these cabs usually charge around 15% more than metered rates, the price is well worth it as these drivers can wait for you while you dine or shop or will pick you up when you call.

Getting Around Safely: Taxis are plentiful, but you may feel more secure having a private car. From Journey Mexico at www.journeymexico.com

Metered Taxis

Some sitio taxis (radio taxis) are safe and use meters, others have fixed rates. Travelers need to be cautious as some drivers will overcharge passengers, advance the meter, or even drive farther than requested to run up the tab.

Do not hail a taxi. A lot of the drivers are unlicensed, illegal and unsafe.

Your hotel will call a reputable taxi for you, a "radio taxi." If you're in a restaurant and ready to leave at night, have them call a cab for you.

If you're out on the street and need a cab, go into a nearby hotel or restaurant and have them call for you. Or go to a taxi stand, labeled *Sitio de Taxi,* where real tcxis will be located. These are designated taxis and OK to use. These maroon and gold Nissans are slightly more expensive than the green *libre* taxis, but much more secure.

Metro

The Mexico City subway offers one of the cheapest fares in the world and has twelve lines that cover the entire city. The Metro is open Monday – Friday (5 a.m. to midnight), Saturday (6 a.m. to midnight), and Sunday (7 a.m. to midnight). The

Metro is very crowded during the day and traveling during rush hours should be avoided. Tickets are sold at the ticket booth in each station. After passing through the turnstile, look for two large signs showing the destinations and follow the signs. Make sure you know where you are going as there is only one map with the routes at the entrance of the station. Note: SALIDA means EXIT and ANDENES means PLATFORMS. Once you get on the train, there's a map of the station stops for that line only located above each door. CORRESPONDENCIAS means transfer points. Be prepared to walk a bit inside the Metro system, especially when transferring lines. **Remember, this is not the safest way to travel and Metro pickpockets prey on tourists.**

Bus

Traveling by bus is common for locals. However, visitors should beware. There are bus stops on all the major tourist streets and most post a map with the full route description. The Metrobus, introduced in 2006, runs in its own designated lane up and down Avenida Insurgentes and usually travels faster than the surrounding traffic. Most of these buses are used by commuters but if you know where you're going and know the stop, the Metrobus is a better alternative to the other buses.

Microbuses

Some tourists like to use the peseros (microbuses); these are sedans or minibuses that run along major roadways. These buses have established fares and pick up and let off passengers along the route and usually offer a more comfortable ride and speedy journey. These microbuses are usually green and gray and display cards in the windshield with their routes. As the bus nears a stop, the driver will put his hand out the wind displaying one or more fingers indicating the number of passengers he can accommodate.

Tourist Bus

Many cities feature the red double-decker hop-on and hop-off tour buses (in Mexico City they are called **Turibuses;** www.turibus.com.mx and here in Mexico City they offer different tours in the north and south of the city. Each bus seats 75 and offers an audio tour in five languages. These buses operate from 9 a.m. to 9 p.m. and for a set fee tourists can hop-on and hop off as often as desired. One of their most popular tours is the Chapultepec-Centro Histórico route with 25 stops including major monuments, museums and neighborhoods. Another favorite circuit takes passengers from La Roma neighborhood south with stops that include the World Trade Center, Plaza de Torros bullring, Carillo Gil museum, Perisur shopping center, and the Frida Kahlo museum. Another tour route goes to the pyramids at Teotihuacán.

Rental Car

If you are traveling without a car and want to travel to Puebla or other surrounding areas, you may consider a rental car. Be warned that due to the high percentage of auto theft, **renting a car in Mexico City is not recommended**.

Do not rent a car unless you're familiar with the area. These people drive like maniacs. The last thing you want is to be in a fender bender in this country where bribes are so common. If you're not prepared to deal with the police, avoid renting a car.

It is not advised to drive in the city if you're not familiar with the streets and neighborhoods, especially if you don't read Spanish, as all the signs are in Spanish, and you certainly don't want to take the chance of landing in one of the city's unsavory neighborhoods. One safe option is to hire a car with a driver—Avis offers chauffeur-driven rental cars at all of its Mexico City locations –the drivers know the area and are great tour guides. (Avis – 800-352-7900 in the U.S. or 1-800-288-8888 in Mexico).

Chapter 3
WHERE TO STAY

CONDESA DF
Avenue Veracruz 102, Col., 52 55 5241-2600
www.condesadf.com/main.html
NEIGHBORHOOD: Condesa
This is definitely one of the top places you will want
to consider staying in because it's new and hip and
attracts a trendy crowd not only as guests, but to its

charming public spaces. Paris designer India Mahdavi took over this 1920s French Neoclassical style building and jumped it up with turquoise walls and ultra-modern furnishings. The outside of the building is distinguished and stately. Inside, it's a crazy wonderful colorful surprise. They offer 40 rooms arrayed around a courtyard in the center. The place is decorated with alpaca carpets, Oaxacan blankets, dark wood paneling and other fun items. The Condesa neighborhood is home to numerous art galleries and fun, stimulating shops, so this place also makes an excellent stop for a drink after you've done some exploring and shopping. (Get the cucumber mezcal mojito made with mezcal blanco by Los Danzantes of Oaxaca.) If you're visiting in the spring, you'll love the blooming jacaranda trees with purple flowers surrounding the rooftop terrace where there's also a sushi bar. In the basement at night there's a dance club where it goes on till late.

DOWNTOWN MEXICO HOTEL

Isabel La Católica 30, Mexico City, +52 55 5282 2199
www.downtownmexico.com
NEIGHBORHOOD: Downtown/Historical District
This hotel combines Colonial 17th century grandeur with a modern twist. Next to Colonial landmarks on a cobbled street, this hotel is located in the central balcony of the Palace of the Countess of Miravalle. In a unique setting filled with art, guests can enjoy breakfast. The large terrace offers great views of the historic churches, Torre Latinoamericana and the Casino Espanol. The owners, Grupo Habita, have

elegantly combined the old structure with modern touches, like the bar and pool on the rooftop that attracts a fun crowd. Be sure to explore the mezzanine where there are carefully selected shops selling mescal, pottery from the provinces and rich chocolates. Amenities include: Flat screen TVs, Bigelow Apothecaries, dry cleaning, Wi-Fi, and room service.

FOUR SEASONS HOTEL MEXICO, D.F.
Paseo de la Reforma 500, Mexico City, +52 55 5230 1818
www.fourseasons.com/mexico/
NEIGHBORHOOD: Cuauhtémoc
Located near Chapultepec Park, this beautiful hotel has a staff as smooth as any you'll find in any Four Seasons hotel around the world. You get the feel of Colonial times in the lobby and rooms, as well as the courtyard, its fountain offering a soothing respite

from the din outside. The hotel offers 240 elegantly appointed guest rooms, including 40 suites. Amenities include: LCD flat-screen TVs, free wireless high-speed Internet access, heated outdoor pool, spa, and fitness center. On-site restaurant, **Reforma 500**, offers Latin American cuisine and lunch and/or cocktails are available at **El Bar**. Around the corner from the hotel entrance, on Calle Burdeos, you'll find street-side vendors selling really good tacos and other street food.

INTERCONTINENTAL PRESIDENTE MEXICO CITY

Campos Elíseos 218, Polanco, Polanco IV Secc, 11560 Ciudad de México, CDMX, +52 55 5327 7700
www.ihg.com/intercontinental/hotels/gb/en/reservatio
n
NEIGHBORHOOD: Federal District / Polanco
Overlooking Chapultepec Park, this modern high-rise (42 floors) hotel offers 661 guest rooms and suites. From the higher floors you get a magnificent view of the mountains that encircle the city (when the air isn't terribly polluted, which is not often). Depending on your rate, you'll probably get a buffet breakfast included with you room. You'll find it to be heads and shoulders above most such buffets, with eggs made to order, lots of pastries. There are 5 or 6 restaurants on site, including an outpost of New York's steakhouse, the **Palm**, **Chapulin** (serving Mexican cuisine), an import from Paris, the bistro **Au Pied de Cochon**, which actually does a great job of replicating the bistro atmosphere they have in Paris; the trattoria **Alfredo di Roma**, that has a nice outdoor

terrace. Once I was here on a whirlwind 4-day trip working on a movie script and the producers put me up here. I was holed up, never able to leave the room except occasionally. I spent time in all these restaurants and was very satisfied. Amenities: Wi-Fi (surcharge), flat-screen TVs, iPod docks and coffeemakers. Hotel facilities: cocktail lounge, health club & spa, ballroom, and indoor swimming pool. Conveniently located near National Museum of Anthropology, Ruth Lechuga Museum and Paseo de la Reforma, which has lots of buses and numerous cabs.

LA CASONA
Durango 280, Cuauhtémoc, Mexico City, +52 55 5286 3001
www.hotellacasona.com.mx

NEIGHBORHOOD: Federal District
With its central location, this small, cozy hotel offers
guests 29 exclusive guest rooms. Amenities include:
free 10Mb Fibreoptic Internet, flat screen TV with
cable, safe deposit boxes, writing desk, room service,
air conditioning, and snack basket. No smoking
rooms available. Facilities include: Restaurant, bar,
reading room, gymnasium and steam room. Bicycles
available for guests.

LA VALISE
Tonalá 53, Mexico City, 52-55-5965-2585
www.lavalise.com
NEIGHBORHOOD: Roma
Probably the hottest, hippest place in all Mexico City
is Roma, loaded with shops, restaurants and bars, but
few hotels. However, there's a great little lodging
owned by French ex-patriot designer Emmanuel

Picault, who opened a few rooms above his distinctive shop in a building dating back to the 1920s on a street lined with trees. Picault, originally from Normandy, has designed interiors for the local **Chic by Accident** (a trendy shop) and also a local nightclub, **M. N. Roy** (in a subterranean space behind a rundown ice cream parlor, also in Roma), as well as Nüba, one of the better nightclubs in Paris. The décor in the 3 rooms he offers for rent here are very modern, but reflect his appreciation of Mesoamerican art of the Mayans and Aztecs. There's a hammock strung up in the atrium, adding a whimsical touch. Each of the 3 suites offer different takes on black-and-white, while the outside of the building reflects an ornate Beaux-Arts look. There's no restaurant, but one of the best restaurants in the city is nearby, **Rosetta**, and waiters will come over with breakfast, lunch or dinner if you ask them.

LAS ALCOBAS
Presidente Masaryk 390, Mexico City, +52 55 3300 3900

www.lasalcobas.com
NEIGHBORHOOD: Federal District
Located in one of the most exclusive neighborhoods
of Mexico City, his masterfully designed boutique
hotel offers 35 guest rooms, suites and penthouses.
Most of the residences offer wraparound terraces and
all feature state of the art technology. The hotel
features in room spa facilities, rain showers, and
Jacuzzi. Facilities include on-site restaurant and spa.

LIVE AQUA BOSQUES
Paseo de Los Tamarindos 98, Mexico City, +52 55
9177 8400
www.liveaqua.com
NEIGHBORHOOD: Bosques de las Lomas
This unique and innovative hotel offers a relaxed
ambiance in a luxury setting. Now, bear in mind that
it's about an hour outside downtown in the Santa Fe
neighborhood, but it attracts a good clientele. The
hotel offers 114 luxurious guest rooms and 23 suites.

Amenities include: 46-inch Smart TV, Nespresso coffeemaker, and motorized drapes. Every floor has its own concierge. On-site restaurant and Spa.

RED TREE HOUSE
Culiacan 6, Mexico City, +52 55 5584 3829
www.theredtreehouse.com
NEIGHBORHOOD: Federal District
This is Mexico City's top B&B. You'll get personal service and lots of hospitality. This is not a luxury hotel but the rooms are tasteful with beautiful surroundings. Amenities include: free wireless Internet and a free breakfast. Conveniently located near parks, restaurants, art galleries, shopping, and city transportation.

ST REGIS
Paseo de la Reforma 439, Mexico City, 52 55 5228 1818

NEIGHBORHOOD: Cuauhtemoc
Located in the first 15 floors of the sleek, 31-story
Torre Libertad (designed by Cesar Pelli), the St.
Regis Mexico City overlooks the Paseo de la

Reforma. The luxury hotel offers 189 large and very
plush rooms, including 36 suites and a grand
presidential suite. Amenities include: Remede bath
amenities, GDA system for master control, oversized
flat screen TVs, CD/DVD player, and in-room digital
movie system. Wi-Fi Internet Access available. Hotel
facilities include: King Cole Bar and a Spa and
Fitness Center from which there happens to be one of
the best views in the whole city.

**St Regis (center above) and the
King Cole Bar (below)**

Chapter 4
WHERE TO EAT

One good thing about eating in Mexico City is that it's possible to eat cheaply here from one end of town to the other. The street food is really terrific, maybe the best in the world except for certain cities in Southeast Asia. Every corner will have great food on it.

TOURS-FOOD
CLUB TENGO HAMBRE
https://clubtengohambre.com/
If you find exploring the fascinating topic of Mexican cuisine a little on the daunting side, you won't be the

first one to grapple with some basic fears. Should I drink the water? (Only if it's bottled.) Should I eat the food? This latter question is especially pertinent when it comes to the famous "street food" one finds on every corner in this sprawling city. A great way to deal with this, and have some fun as well, is to take one of the tours offered by this company. You'll have some wonderful experiences, and you won't be afraid to eat the food. Besides the food, you'll get an insider's guide to the city.

MEXICO CITY STREET FOOD ESSENTIALS
This walking tour takes about 3 ½ hours and makes 6 stops. They insist the places they stop to eat will serve food only available here in the city, and not in other places in the country. Interesting, right?

INSIDER'S GUIDE TO MEXICO CITY'S STREET FOOD – MARKETS + SWEETS + PULQUE
This walking tour takes between 3 and 4 hours and makes 6 stops
With this tour, they take you to the best & most interestingly varied food stands downtown, as well as markets, panaderias, confectioneries, and introduce you to pulque, which is a milk-colored drink that goes back centuries and packs a real punch. It's the fermented juice of the maguey plant (the agave plant—the blue agave is used to make tequila). It looks somewhat off-putting (even disgusting), but after the second one, you'll grow to love it. LOL.

MEXICO CITY AFTER DARK

This walking tour takes about 3 ½ hours and makes 7 stops. I really enjoyed this one, because I don't like to go out too late by myself, but this was great fun. Some food stands are best at night, and I've never had better tacos, anywhere, period. They also take you to an historic cantina and a pulqueria where you can really get soused.

AMAYA

Calle Gral. Prim 95, +01 55 5592 5671
http://www.amayamexico.com/
CUISINE: International
DRINKS: Full Bar
SERVING: Lunch & Dinner
PRICE RANGE: $$$
NEIGHBORHOOD: Juárez

Lovely little place with high ceilings and Aztec / Mayan murals painted over old red brick walls that definitely give the eatery a certain charm. A small bar has a handful of seats where you can also eat. Small but complex menu featuring dishes like: Lamp pita, Soft shell crab, and Tuna ceviche. Nice wine list focusing on natural wines. Excellent Vegetarian options.

AZUL CONDESA
Nuevo León 68, Cuauhtémoc, Hipódromo, Mexico City, +52-55-5286-6380
www.azul.rest
CUISINE: Mexican
DRINKS: Full Bar
SERVING: Breakfast, Lunch
PRICE RANGE: $$$
NEIGHBORHOOD: Condesa

Chef Ricardo Munoz Zurita offers a menu of authentic Mexican cuisine in a simple atmosphere of wooden tables and chairs. Though the dining room is electric with activity, try to get one of the tables in the atrium garden if you can swing it. Very lush and tropical. Menu favorites include: Beef drizzled in a smoky Oaxacan mole, Veracruz style fish, and ancient Mayan dishes. Try the "enigmatico" chichilo negro, which is one of the 7 Oaxaca moles you seldom see. (It's made with chihuacle pepper ashes and is usually served with beef.)

AZUL HISTÓRICO

Isabel la Católica, 30, Centro Historico A, 52 55 5510 1316
www.azul.rest
CUISINE: Mexican
DRINKS: Full Bar
SERVING: Brunch, Lunch, Dinner
PRICE RANGE: $$$
NEIGHBORHOOD: Downtown south / Centro Sur
With lights in the thick-branched trees overhead, you couldn't find a more romantic spot than this popular restaurant serving favorites like Stuffed Duck Fritters dipped in mole and Black Chichilo Chiluacle Chili served with venison. This is also a great place for breakfast, serving favorites like chilaquiles, Mexican eggs, and enchiladas. Try the delicious house-made chocolate cake served with gorgonzola cheese ice cream.

BELMONDO
Tabasco 109, Mexico City, +55 62 73 2079
www.belmondo.com.mx/
CUISINE: Deli, Sandwiches
DRINKS: Wines
SERVING: Lunch & Dinner
PRICE RANGE: $
NEIGHBORHOOD: Roma Norte
This eatery draws lots of young creative and trendy
types and offers a simple menu featuring salads,
sandwiches as spot on and good as any you've had
anywhere. Also a curated list of wines by the glass.
Menu favorites include: the French dip with roast
beef and gravy, or the grilled cheese with caramelized
onions. Closed Sundays. Be prepared for a wait.

BÓSFORO
Luis Moya 31, Mexico City, +52 55 5512 1991

No Website
CUISINE: Mexican
DRINKS: Full Bar
SERVING: Breakfast, Lunch, Dinner
PRICE RANGE: $$
NEIGHBORHOOD: Federal District
This small friendly neighborhood bar specializes in mezcales and offers a menu of Mexican bar food with favorites like the quesadilla and tapas. Try the desserts especially if you're a chocolate lover.

CABRERA 7
Calle Plaza Luis Cabrera 7, Miguel Hidalgo, Mexico City, 52 55 5264 4531
CUISINE: Mexican
DRINKS: Full Bar
SERVING: Brunch, Lunch, Dinner

PRICE RANGE: $$
NEIGHBORHOOD: Roma Norte
This superb two-level restaurant and lounge bar (overlooking the gorgeous fountains decorating **Plaza Luis Cabrera**), and has a menu featuring Mexican cuisine from all regions. Menu favorites include: Oaxacan mole, cochinita pibil, and of course the tacos and tortas. This place makes for great people-watching as artists set up makeshift stalls to sell their wares and the whole population flows by in a continuous and colorful parade of humanity.

CAFÉ EL POPULAR RESTAURANTE
5 de Mayo, No. 50-52, Mexico City, 55 5518-6081
CUISINE: Cafe
DRINKS: No Booze
SERVING: 24 hours
PRICE RANGE: $$
NEIGHBORHOOD: Central Historic District
This 24-hour café offers great Mexican breakfast like huevos rancheros or enchiladas verdes under a wood beamed ceiling. Great coffees and pastries. If you're lucky there will be live music.

CAFÉ NIN
Calle Havre 73, Juárez, Mexico, +52 55 9155 4805
www.cafenin.com.mx
CUISINE: Breakfast
DRINKS: No Booze
SERVING: Breakfast
PRICE RANGE: $$
NEIGHBORHOOD: Juárez

Great choice for breakfast and the most popular brunch spot in the area. Impressive selection of baked goods – everything from doughnuts to croissants and the best-ever guava cheese pastries. Delicious cappuccino. Nice small plates as well, like the avocado & squid ceviche.

CAFÉ PASSMAR
Calle Adolfo Prieto s/n Local 237, Mexico City, +52 55 5669 1994
www.cafepassmar.com
CUISINE: Cafeteria/Coffeehouse
NEIGHBORHOOD: Benito Juárez
Just a coffeehouse that offers a full range of coffees beyond Starbucks presentation along with fruit smoothies, herbal teas, and frappes.

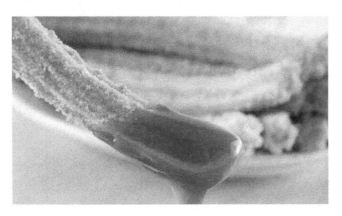

CHURRERÍA EL MORO
Several Locations (more listed on web site)
Eje Central Lázaro Cárdenas 42, Centro +52 55 5512 0896

Calle Río Lerma 167, Col. Cuauhtémoc + 52 55 5512 0896
Mercado Roma, Querétaro 225
Av. Michoacán 27, Col. Condesa
https://elmoro.mx/
CUISINE: Churros
DRINKS: No Booze
SERVING: 24 hours (some locations hours vary)
PRICE RANGE: $
NEIGHBORHOOD: Histórico, Centro / Roma Norte / Centro Sur / Condesa / Cuauhtémoc
Churros, churros, churros. Beautifully designed bakeries—light, bright and cheerful—(though the decor changes from one location to another) featuring churros, which is basically just plain dough fried and sugared. Originating in Portugal and Spain, churros are a mainstay snack here in Mexico and a lot of other Latin countries. They have to be eaten when they're warm to be fully appreciated. Here at this bakery, where they do things the old-fashioned way, they make 'em to order, so you get fresh churros with a variety of toppings, everything from deep dark chocolate to dulce de leche. Try the churro ice cream sandwiches. Impressive selection of hot chocolates.

CONTRAMAR
Calle de Durango 200, Mexico City, +52 55 5514 9217
www.contramar.com.mx
CUISINE: Seafood
DRINKS: Full Bar
SERVING: Lunch, Dinner
PRICE RANGE: $$$

NEIGHBORHOOD: Condesa
This seafood restaurant is considered one of the chicest dining halls in the whole country, and not so much for its food, which is fine, but for the eclectic mix of artists, hipsters and trendy types it attracts. Blue and white color scheme highlights the high-ceilinged room. Best people-watching in the city. Has a great selection of dishes, including Tuna Tostadas, Oysters & pescado a la talla, Crab Cakes, and Spaghetti with Clams.

COOX HANAL
Calle Isabel la Catolica 83, Centro Histórico, Centro, 06090 Ciudad de México, CDMX,
+52 55 5709 3613
www.cooxhanal.com
CUISINE: Mexican
DRINKS: Full bar
SERVING: Lunch & Dinner
PRICE RANGE: $$$
NEIGHBORHOOD: Central Historic District
Popular eatery (since 1953) on the second floor offering authentic Yucatan fare like *poc chuc* (pork grilled after being marinated in orange juice). Other menu picks: Chamorro and Lime soup. Live music. This place was originally opened by boxer Raul Salazar, from Yucatan's capital, Merida.

DELIRIO
Ave. Monterrey 116-b, Mexico City, +52 55 5584 0870
www.delirio.mx
CUISINE: French/Deli
DRINKS: Beer & Wine Only
SERVING: Breakfast, Lunch & Dinner; closed Mon
PRICE RANGE: $$
NEIGHBORHOOD: Roma Norte
Great place to stop if you're looking for non-Mexican fare. Light dishes like focaccia.

DULCE PATRIA
Anatole France 100, Mexico City, 52 55 3300 3999
www.dulcepatriamexico.com
CUISINE: Mexican
DRINKS: Full Bar
SERVING: Breakfast, Lunch
PRICE RANGE: $$$$
NEIGHBORHOOD: Polanco
Chef Martha Ortiz offers a menu of traditional
Mexican cuisine with a modern twist. It's her
innovative approach that has pushed her to the
forefront of the "New Mexican" cuisine that's
exploding all over the country (and abroad). This 90-
seat eatery features two terraces inside the restaurant
giving an outdoor feel. Definitely begin with her
ceviche. But also try her fabulous "sangritas" as a
chaser after you down a shot of tequila.

EL CARDENAL
Palma 23, México, D.F., +52 55 5521 8815

www.restauranteelcardenal.com
CUISINE: Mexican
DRINKS: Full Bar
SERVING: Breakfast, Lunch, & Dinner
PRICE RANGE: $$
NEIGHBORHOOD: Centro Sur
Located in a beautiful old house, this popular eatery serves authentic Mexican fare. Favorites: Quesadillas with guac, and Chicken with nopales. Popular brunch spot. If you're there for one of the best breakfast in town, get the *huevos en caldo de frijol.*

EL FAROLITO
Altata 19, Col. Condesa, México, D.F., +52-55-5273-0142
www.taqueriaselfarolito.com.mx
CUISINE: Tacos
DRINKS: No Booze
SERVING: Lunch & Dinner
PRICE RANGE: $
NEIGHBORHOOD: Condesa
Delicious Mexican fare prepared right in front of you at this decades-old spot with several locations. Try the Faroladas de Bisteck (Pita bread with steak and cheese). Nice selection of fruit juices.

EL HIDALGUENSE
Campeche 155, Mexico City, +52 55 5564 0538
No Website
CUISINE: Mexican
DRINKS: No Booze
SERVING: Open only 7 a.m. – 5 p.m. Fri - Sun
PRICE RANGE: $$

NEIGHBORHOOD: Roma Sur
A locals' favorite, this Mexican eatery offers a great
selection of barbecue, meats, montalayo, and seafood.
Authentic Mexican fare.

EL MAYOR
Républica de Argentina 15, Col. Centro, Mexico City,
52 55 5704 7580
www.restaurantelmayor.com.mx
CUISINE: Mexican
DRINKS: Full Bar
SERVING: Brunch, Lunch
PRICE RANGE: $$
NEIGHBORHOOD: Centro Histórico
Located on the top floor above a bookstore, this
modern restaurant offers a menu of Mexican favorites
and European-influenced fusion dishes. This is also a

great place for brunch. There's a rooftop bar that overlooks the ruins of the Aztec city.

EL TURIX
Emilio Castelar, 212, Mexico City, 52 55 5280 6449
CUISINE: Mexican
DRINKS: Beer & Wine
SERVING: Lunch, Dinner
PRICE RANGE: $
NEIGHBORHOOD: Colonia Polanco
Located in a dingy storefront, but the food is worth the visit. There's an outdoor patio and a couple tables inside. Menu favorites include Cochinita pibil (pork slowly cooked with achiote that is a specialty of the Yucatán) and Tamales.

EL VENADITO
Universidad 1701, Col. Chimalistac, México, D.F.,
+52 55 5661 9786
No Web Site
CUISINE: Tacos
DRINKS: Beer &Wine
SERVING: Lunch & Dinner
PRICE RANGE: $
NEIGHBORHOOD: Florida
For over 50 years this place has served typical
Mexican fare to lines of happy customers. Known for
their great Carnitas. Favorites: Enchiladas, tacos al
pastor and French toast dessert. Across the street you
can see the Chapel of San Jose del Atillo.

ENO
Francisco Petrarca 258, Mexico City, +52 55 5531
8535
www.eno.com.mx
CUISINE: Sandwiches
DRINKS: Beer & Wine Only
SERVING: Breakfast, Lunch & Dinner
PRICE RANGE: $$
NEIGHBORHOOD: Polanco
Casual eatery that specializes in sandwiches. Great
spot for breakfast or lunch. Seating is communal.
Favorites include the carnitas de atun (seared tuna)
sandwich.

FLOR DE LIS
Avenida Mazatlan 30, Condesa, Mexico City, 52 55
5211 0060
www.tamalesyatole.com

CUISINE: Mexican
DRINKS: Beer & Wine
SERVING: Dinner
PRICE RANGE: $
NEIGHBORHOOD: Condesa
If you're looking for tamales, this is your place.
There's a nice variety including chicken, peppers,
beef, mole, and sweet (fruit). The atmosphere is
quaint but the food is solid. Menu favorites included
the Chicken and tomato tamale wrapped in banana
leaf.

FONDA MARGARITA
Adolfo Prieto 1364, Mexico City, +52 55 5559 6358
CUISINE: Mexican
DRINKS: No Booze
SERVING: Breakfast, Lunch & Dinner
PRICE RANGE: $

NEIGHBORHOOD: Benito Juarez
Authentic Mexican cuisine typical of the region. Try the chicharrones in green sauce served with fresh tortillas and eggs and beans. Very few vegetarian options. Spanish speaking only.

FONDA MAYORA
Campeche 322, Hipódromo, Mexico City, +52 55 6843 0595
www.fondamayora.com
CUISINE: Mexican
DRINKS: Full bar
SERVING: Breakfast, Lunch & Dinner (early)
PRICE RANGE: $$$
NEIGHBORHOOD: Condesa
Chef Gerardo Vázquez Lugo offers a menu of traditional Mexican fare. The best was the guacamole served from a cart and mixed to order with your choice of onions, tomatoes, and avocado. Everything is served fresh. Not a tourist destination.

HAVRE 77
Havre 77, Col. Juárez, México, D.F., 5208 1070
No Website
CUISINE: French-Mexican
DRINKS: No Booze
SERVING: Breakfast, Lunch; closed Mon & Tues
PRICE RANGE: $$$$
NEIGHBORHOOD: Juárez
Small eatery reminiscent of cafes in Paris. A perfect place to stop when you want a break from Mexican food. Favorites: Steak frites, Escargots du Jour and

Laitue (salad with fresh tarragon). Delicious French pastries make this a nice stop early in the morning.

HOSTERIA DE SANTO DOMINGO
Calle Belisario Dominguez 72, 06010 México, D.F., +52 55 5526 5276
No Website
CUISINE: Mexican
DRINKS: Full bar
SERVING: Breakfast, Lunch & Dinner
PRICE RANGE: $$
NEIGHBORHOOD: Centro Norte
Traditional authentic Mexican fare in the city's oldest restaurant that opened in the 1860s. Gourmet dishes featuring meats and fish, like the *chile en nogado*, large poblano chile peppers stuffed full of ground meat, dried fruit and topped with a rich, creamy sauce. Live music. The atmosphere may remind you of your grandmother's house, or, come to think of it, your great-grandmother's house.

GUZINA OAXACA
Masaryk 513, Mexico City**, +52 55 5282 1820**

CUISINE: Mexican
DRINKS: Full bar
SERVING: Breakfast, Lunch & Dinner
PRICE RANGE: $$
NEIGHBORHOOD: Polanco
Chef Alejandro Ruíz recently opened this location of his acclaimed Oaxaca eatery serving contemporary Mexican fare. Here you'll get delicious homemade tortillas, tableside served Oaxacan salsa, and mole. Great choice for breakfast. Make reservations for this place.

LA BARRACA VALENCIANA
Centenario 91-C, Col. Del Carmen, Mexico City, +52 55 5658 1880
www.labarracavalenciana.com

CUISINE: Spanish/Tapas/Small Plates
DRINKS: Beer & Wine Only
SERVING: Lunch & Dinner; closed Sun
PRICE RANGE: $$
NEIGHBORHOOD: Coyoacán
Small eatery (only 12 tables) serving a menu of tapas and small plates. Favorites include: Squid Roman, Grilled chicken breast and Chamorro veal. Specials change weekly.

LA CASA DE LAS SIRENAS
Calle Republica de Guatemala No. 32 Centro Histórico, Mexico City, 52 55 5593 4916
www.tortaslacastellana.com
CUISINE: Continental
DRINKS: Full Bar
SERVING: Breakfast, Lunch, Dinner
PRICE RANGE: $$$
NEIGHBORHOOD: Centro Histórico (Central Historic)
This charming restaurant overlooks the Cathedral of Mexico City and the National Palace. Menu favorites include: Roast chicken and Rib Eye. Delicious desserts. The restaurant features a tequila salon with dozens of agave spirits and a rooftop with tables that look into the cathedral's garden.

LA CASA DE TOÑO
Several Locations
Londres 144, + 52 55 5386 1125
https://m.lacasadetono.com.mx/
CUISINE: Mexican
DRINKS: Beer & Wine

SERVING: Open 24 hours (some vary)
PRICE RANGE: $
NEIGHBORHOOD: Juarez
Mexican diner open 24 hours. Very basic décor, nothing fancy. Large menu. Famous for its Pozole (which is a soup or stew with a base of hominy and mixed with meat (most often pork) and then finished off with seasonings and cabbage, lettuce, chili peppers, onion, garlic, radishes, avocado, or whatever they happen to decide that day. It's really flavorful. But the menu is quite vast—enchiladas, quesadillas, cochinita tacos, flan, rice pudding. Favorites: Pozole and Horchata. Mexican beers.

LA CASTELLANA
AV Revolucion 1309 esq Corregidora, Mexico City, 52 55 5593 5711
www.grupocastellano.com.mx
CUISINE: Mexican
DRINKS: Beer & Wine
SERVING: Lunch, Dinner
PRICE RANGE: $
Specializing in tortas, this is just one of five locations. The tortas are made with crisp-crusted and light bread, pickled jalapenos and a variety of fillings. And cheap, cheap, cheap.

LA DOCENA OYSTER BAR
Av. Álvaro Obregón 31, Mexico City, +52 55 5208
0833
www.ladocena.com.mx
CUISINE: Seafood
DRINKS: Full bar
SERVING: Lunch & Dinner
PRICE RANGE: $$$
NEIGHBORHOOD: Roma Norte
Seafood eatery specializing in oysters and barbecue.
Favorite dish: Baby squid with garlic. Creative
selection of desserts. Reservations recommended.
English menu available.

LALO!

Calle Zacatecas 173, Mexico City, +52 55 5564 3388
www.eat-lalo.com
CUISINE: Breakfast/Pizza
DRINKS: Beer & Wine Only
SERVING: Breakfast, Lunch & Dinner; Lunch only
on Mon
PRICE RANGE: $$
NEIGHBORHOOD: Roma Norte
Chef Eduardo Garcia's casual eatery just across the
street from his more upscale eatery Maximo Bistrot.
Great choice for breakfast – have the French toast.
Amazing selection of pastries and house-made
yogurt. Dinner choices include dishes like freshly
made octopus with arugula.

LARDO

Agustín Melgar 6, Cuauhtemoc, Mexico City, +52 55
5211 7731
www.lardo.mx
CUISINE: French
DRINKS: Full bar
SERVING: Lunch & Dinner
PRICE RANGE: $$
NEIGHBORHOOD: Condesa
Hip eatery with a menu of Mexican and international
cuisine. Great selection of seafood and seasonal
dishes. They will even make dishes to order. Nice
selection of wines.

LAS CAZUELAS DE LA ABUELA

Av San Jeronimo 630, Mexico City, +52 55 5683
8720
https://las-cazuelas-de-la-abuela.business.site
CUISINE: Mexican
DRINKS: Full Bar
SERVING: Dinner
PRICE RANGE: $
NEIGHBORHOOD: Pedregal
This family restaurant offers a menu of Mexican
cuisine with Poblano overtones. The menu features 25
different stews and delicious peneques – a deep-fried
quesadilla with green and red pumpkin-seed sauce.

LIMOSNEROS

Av. Ignacio Allende 3, Col. Centro Histórico, +52 55 5521 5576

http://limosneros.com.mx/

CUISINE: Mexican

DRINKS: Full Bar

SERVING: Lunch & Dinner

PRICE RANGE: $$$

NEIGHBORHOOD: Centro Norte

Upscale eatery offering Mexican cuisine with an international twist. The interior walls look like they were patched together using ancient stones. These walls are high and very dramatic. Interesting clear glass light fixtures dangle delicately from the high ceiling. Pots and vases on a shelf look like someone had a field day at a potter's shop. The lighting at night makes the place quite romantic. Bottles behind the bar are balanced (some of them precariously) on odd-shaped stone shelves. Has a menu including tacos, lamb, steak, Squid risotto and Crème Brule. My favorites: the steak tacos. Nice wine list and tasty cocktails.

LOS PANCHOS
Calle Tolstoi 9, Miguel Hidalgo, +52 55 5254 5430
www.lospanchos.mx
CUISINE: Mexican
DRINKS: Full bar
SERVING: Breakfast, Lunch & Dinner
PRICE RANGE: $$
NEIGHBORHOOD: Anzures
Great place for a family dinner.
Traditional Mexican eatery that's worth a try. Great dishes and the steak here is exceptional (not your typical American steak). Nice selection of desserts.

MAISON ARTEMISIA
Tonalá 23, Cuauhtémoc, Mexico City, +52 55 6303 2471
www.maisonartemisia.com
CUISINE: French
DRINKS: Full bar
SERVING: Lunch & Dinner; closed Sun
PRICE RANGE: $$$
NEIGHBORHOOD: Roma Norte
Upscale dining with an upstairs piano bar. Restaurant offers a nice selection of seafood and beef. Favorites include: Grilled octopus and Short-rib ravioli. This place is famous for its imported absinthe and absinthe-based cocktails.

MAXIMO BISTROT LOCAL
Tonalá 133, Mexico City, 52 55 5264 4291
www.maximobistrot.com.mx
CUISINE: Mexican, Italian, French
DRINKS: Wine
SERVING: Lunch, Dinner
PRICE RANGE: $$$$
NEIGHBORHOOD: Roma Norte
This rustic bistro, run by a young husband-and-wife team, offers a daily menu featuring ingredients found in the local markets. It has an open kitchen and has handwritten daily menus. Menu favorites include: Lamb loin and Tartar of Steelhead. Reservations required.

MERCADO ROMA COYOACAN
Miguel Angel Quevedo 353, Mexicto DF, 55 2155 9435
www.mrc.mercadoroma.com
NEIGHBORHOOD: Coyoacán
Over 40 wildly diverse vendors occupy the 3 floors of this spectacular market, and a lot of them are eateries offering up authentic Mexican fare. While this is basically a collection of upscale food vendors that replicate the down-and-dirty street food you can find all over the city, in this place things are a little tidier, and the excitement stems from the fact that you can sample Mexican-fusion this or that, getting tastes from the far corners of this country. You can get tacos from 9 different regions of the country. But also elements of cuisine from around the world, all blended into Mexicsn cuisince. An Italian vendor serves tacos, but the taco is *piadina*, which is like a

tortilla, but comes from Italy. Hundreds of surprising (and pleasing) combinations like this will enchant you. If you're on a short visit, this place ought to be a must, because you'll get to experience so much so fast.

MERENDERO LAS LUPITAS
Plaza Santa Catarina 4, Col. Del Carmen, México, D.F., +52 55 5554 3353
www.merenderolaslupitas.com.mx/
CUISINE: Mexican
DRINKS: No Booze
SERVING: Breakfast, Lunch; closed Mon & Tues
PRICE RANGE: $$
NEIGHBORHOOD: Coyoacán
Family-run eatery offering authentic Northern Mexican fare. Try the atole (a corn based drink served

hot). Favorites: Chimichangas, egg & bean dishes and Flan.

MERO TORO
Calle Amsterdam 204, Mexico City, +52 55 5564 7799
www.merotoro.mx
CUISINE: Northern Mexican
DRINKS: Full Bar
SERVING: Dinner
PRICE RANGE: $$$
NEIGHBORHOOD: Condesa
Open since 2010, this eatery brings the surf-and-turf cuisine of Baja California to the Mexican highlands. Chef Jair Tellez created the expansive menu. Selections start with the small plate men featuring dishes like Ceviche ligero but don't forget the

delicious main courses like Gently roasted grouper served on a bed of puréed cauliflower.

MOG
Frontera 168, Col. Roma, 52 55 5264 1629
CUISINE: Asian
DRINKS: Beer & Wine Only
SERVING: Lunch, Dinner
PRICE RANGE: $$
NEIGHBORHOOD: Roma Norte
This popular eatery offers a menu of sushi, Japanese style dishes and fusion. The bar serves a variety of Mexican and Japanese beers and sakes. Menu favorites include: Sushi rolls, Teriyaki Chicken and Yakimeshi. Desserts favorites include the green tea cake.

PAPRIKA
Masella 61, Col. Juarez, Mexico City, +52 55 5533 0303
CUISINE: Mediterranean/Moroccan/Arabian
DRINKS: Full bar
SERVING: Lunch & Dinner; closed Sun
PRICE RANGE: $$
NEIGHBORHOOD: Juárez
Middle eastern eatery with a menu of small plate dishes created by Chef Josefina Santacruz. Popular dishes like Lamb and lentils served with rice, pistachios and apricots. Nice menu of teas.

PASTELERÍA IDEAL
Several locations
16 de Septiembre No. 18, +52 55 5130 2970
Republic of Uruguay 74
Av. Hank González 773, Colonia Valle de Aragón
2nd. Sec.
https://www.pasteleriaideal.com.mx/
CUISINE: Bakery
DRINKS: No Booze
SERVING: 6:30 a.m. – 9:30 p.m.
PRICE RANGE: $
NEIGHBORHOOD: Centro Histórico de la Cdad.
Legendary bakery with endless aisles of breads, cookies, croissants, cakes, and a variety of pastries filled with ham & cheese, tuna, and other ingredients. Worth a visit just to absorb the variety available. Plus, it's a lot of fun to try pastry items you've never had before. Eat in or take out. Cheap, too.

PASTELERIA LA GRAN VIA
Amsterdan 288-A, Mexico City, +52 55 5574 4008
www.pastelerialagranvia.com
CUISINE: Bakery/Specialty Grocery
NEIGHBORHOOD: Condesa
Popular bakery featuring a variety of breads, pastries,
doughnuts, cakes and cookies. Great meringues and
low-sugar options.

PUJOL
Tennyson 133, Mexico City, 52 55 5545 4111
www.pujol.com.mx
CUISINE: Mexican/Fusion
DRINKS: Full Bar
SERVING: Brunch, Lunch, Dinner
PRICE RANGE: $$$$
NEIGHBORHOOD: Polanco
With a reputation as one of the world's best
restaurants (and hardest to get into with only a

baker's dozen tables), this Mexican eatery mixes modern (mostly French-inspired) and ancient culinary techniques. Prix-fix menu. Menu favorites include: Fish ceviche taco and Fried pork belly. As an example of Chef Enrique Olvera's innovative culinary talents, I ordered tacos that had baby lamb, avocado-pera purée and the pungently aromatic herb, *hoja santa*. Delicious. This is why Olvera is Mexico's most famous chef.

QUINTONIL
Newton 55, Mexico City, 52 55 5280 1660
www.quintonil.com
CUISINE: Mexican
DRINKS: Full Bar
SERVING: Dinner
PRICE RANGE: $$$
NEIGHBORHOOD: Polanaco
This place takes traditional Mexican cuisine to the next level. Great margaritas and Mexican wines. Menu favorites include: Swiss chard tamale with raison puree; delicate slices of *chilacayote* squash and charred tortillas are topped with mole; *Huauzontle*, which is something similar to broccoli, is fried and served with salsa and cheese from Chiapas.

RESTAURANTE BAR CHON
Regina 160, 06090 México, D.F. +52 55 5542 0873
CUISINE: Mexican; Pre-Hispanic cuisine as well
DRINKS: Full bar
SERVING: Lunch & Dinner; closed Sunday
PRICE RANGE: $$$
NEIGHBORHOOD: Centro Sur

Traditional Mexican fare with most entrees based around the tortilla, rice and beans. This is one of the few places that also serves Pre-Hispanic food, so you can see what it was like to eat before Europeans arrived to muck it all up for the Indians. Unique offerings featuring insects, grasshoppers, worms, ant larvae and wild boar. Try the *pulque* ("blood of the gods"), a flavored beverage. A once-in-a-lifetime experience.

RESTAURANTE NICOS
Av. Cuitlahuac 3102, Mexico City, +52 55 5396 7090
www.nicosmexico.mx
CUISINE: Mexican
DRINKS: Full bar
SERVING: Breakfast, Lunch & Dinner; closed Sun
PRICE RANGE: $$$
NEIGHBORHOOD: Clavería
Not your typical Mexican eatery, great menu of "Nouvelle Mexican cuisine." Imaginative dishes and what many say is the "best" guacamole in the world. If you have a taste for sweets try the chocolate mousse cake. Menu in Spanish but the waiters do a good job of describing the dishes.
Good choice for breakfast.

ROKAI
Rio Ebro 87, Mexico City, 55 5207 7543
http://edokobayashi.com/index.php/rokai/
CUISINE: Japanese
DRINKS: Beer, Wine & Sake
SERVING: Lunch, Dinner; closed Sunday

PRICE RANGE: $
NEIGHBORHOOD: Cuauhtémoc
A favorite among locals and foodies, this small
Japanese eatery serves up famous dishes like Rokai,
mussels sake, tuna, rib eye and duck, red snapper with
Himalayan salt and yuzu paste and Ensenada Octopus
sashimi. They also have a menu with nine or ten
courses –changing daily. They also have a real
standout menu item in their fried chicken. What
makes it different (and a delightful surprise for a
South Carolina boy like myself) is that it's marinated
in sake. The bar offers hot sake, green tea, Sapporo
beer and wine.

SUD777
Blvd. de la Luz 777, Col. Jardines del Pedregal,
México, D.F., +52 55 5568 4777
http://sud777.com.mx
CUISINE: Mexican
DRINKS: Full Bar
SERVING: Breakfast, Lunch, & Dinner
PRICE RANGE: $$$
NEIGHBORHOOD: Jardines del Pedregal
Great dining experience in a classic restaurant open
since 2008 that offers cutting edge innovative cuisine
while relying on traditional Mexican ingredients.
Updated, modern, but still somehow traditional. The
crisscrossing beams above give the place a modern
look, as vines weave in and out of nooks and
crannies. Light brown wooden tables mix with the
blacks and grays to highlight the intimate décor. The
chef swears he never uses any produce that's not
Mexican. (I believe him.) There is a tasting menu,

which I highly recommend. Be sure to get the wine pairing, because this place has one of the best selections of really local Mexican wines to be had in the city. Too many other upscale restaurants focus on foreign labels. Favorites: Tuna tostada with soy, Lechon pork, poblano chiles, Cotija cheese, a foie gras that's made locally and Crab ceviche. (There also a super good sushi bar, **Kokeshi**, tucked away inside this place.)

TABERNA DEL LEON
Altamirano 46, Col.Tizapán San Ángel, 01000
México, D.F., +52 55 5616 2110
CUISINE: Mexican gourmet
DRINKS: Full bar
SERVING: Lunch & Dinner
PRICE RANGE: $$$$
NEIGHBORHOOD: San Angel
Beautiful upscale though casual eatery offering an exceptional dining experience. Favorites: Pork chop with Brussel sprouts and Foie gras; *robalo a los tres chiles* (bass cooked with a three-pepper chili sauce). Excellent desserts like Chocolate cake served with raspberry ice cream.

TACOS DON JUAN
Atlixco 42, 06760 México, D.F., +52 55 5286 0816
No Website
CUISINE: Tacos
DRINKS: No Booze
SERVING: Lunch only
PRICE RANGE: $
NEIGHBORHOOD: La Condesa

Authentic hole-in-the-wall joint offering a rotating menu of fresh tacos. On Sunday, for instance, they'll serve tacos with *bistec con longaniza* (beef with sausage meat) topped off with a dollop of beans; on Friday or Saturday, you'll get *carnitas* (deep-fried pork). It doesn't matter what day you go, though, because every day the tacos are great, which accounts for the lines and why they've been here for so many years. Order at the counter – no inside seating, just outside.

TACOS EL HUEQUITO
Several Locations
Ayuntamiento 21, +52 55 5518 3313
Bolívar 58, Centro
Bajo Puente, Local 4 Esq. Juan Escutia, Col., Condesa
http://www.elhuequito.com.mx/
CUISINE: Mexican
DRINKS: No Booze
SERVING: Breakfast, Lunch, and Dinner
PRICE RANGE: $
NEIGHBORHOOD: Colonia Centro / Condesa
Taco stand located on a side street. Menu includes a variety of salsas and sauces for your tacos. But there's more to the menu—Gringas, Burritos, Nopalitos, Arabs, Aztec Soup, Corn Quesadillas (tasty). Food is served through a small window. Several locations throughout the Central District, some with more generous seating available than the little hole in the wall I generally frequent.

TACOS MANOLO
Luz Saviñón 1305 (bet. Anaxágoras and Cauhtémoc),
Mexico City, 52 55 5687 5923
No Website
CUISINE: Mexican
DRINKS:
SERVING: Lunch, Dinner
PRICE RANGE: $$
NEIGHBORHOOD: Colonia Del Valle
This busy stand is all about tacos. Try the classic
Manolo, chopped bistec with onion and bacon.

TAQUERIA EL CALIFA
Altata 22, Mexico City, +52 55 5271 7666
www.elcalifa.com.mx
CUISINE: Mexican
DRINKS: Beer & Wine
SERVING: Dinner
PRICE RANGE: $$
NEIGHBORHOOD: Condesa

A popular taqueria with traditional favorites like the chicharon de queso and the Gaona conqueso.

TAQUERIA EL PROGRESO
Calle Maestro Antonio Caso 30, Col. Tabacalera,
+52 55 5546 4700
https://taqueriaelprogreso.negocio.site/
CUISINE: Tacos
DRINKS: No Booze
SERVING: Breakfast, Lunch; closed Mon & Tues
PRICE RANGE: $
NEIGHBORHOOD: Tabacalera
Tacos at this great little sidewalk café are served with a variety of meats and lots of toppings including mashed potatoes, beans, cactus, manzanita peppers and onions. Cow head tacos served here (tacos de cabeza), as well as the excellent cow brain. (Check out the juice bar next door.)

TAQUERIA LOS COCUYOS
Calle Bolívar 56, Mexico City, 52 55 5518 4231

No Website
CUISINE: Tacos
DRINKS: Full Bar
SERVING: Lunch, Dinner
PRICE RANGE: $
NEIGHBORHOOD: Centro
This little taqueria offers up an interesting menu of
tacos. Bright lights illuminate the different cuts of
meat in a huge pan jammed with God knows what.
You'd never stop at a place like this ordinarily. It's so
small, so cramped, so scary looking. But it's the
BEST. (The smell is so wonderful.) You tell them
what you want and they cut the meat to order to make
some of the best tacos you'll ever taste. And cheap,
cheap, cheap. You eat standing in the street. Menu
favorites include: Suadero (braised and seared beef)
and Beef tongue taco.

TETETLAN
Av. de Las Fuentes 180, Col. Jardines del Pedregal,
Ciudad de México, +52 55 5668 5335
www.tetetlan.com
CUISINE: Mexican
DRINKS: Full Bar
SERVING: Breakfast, Lunch, & Dinner
PRICE RANGE: $$
NEIGHBORHOOD: Pedregal
Located off the beaten path is this ultra-trendy eatery,
that uses many different kinds of stone in its walls,
rocks, bricks, poured concrete. Lots of weird angles,
nooks and crannies. Completely charming. The name
of this place actually means "place of many stones."
You'll love it. They offer a menu of international and

regional cuisine, boasting that over 90% of what they use comes from Mexico. Favorites: Roasted huitlacoche (this is a fungus that grows on corn), dried crickets with lemon and Tamales with hoja santa. Nice selection of tequilas.

TORTAS EL CAPRICHO
Augusto Rodin, 407, Mexico City, 52 55 5563 9158
CUISINE: Mexican
DRINKS: Beer & Wine
SERVING: Lunch, Dinner
PRICE RANGE: $
NEIGHBORHOOD: Colonia Mixoac
This eatery, very popular among the locals, specializes in tortas, large cake sandwiches, and offers nearly 50 varieties.

YUBAN
Colima 268, Mexico City, 52 55 6387 0358
www.yuban.mx
CUISINE: Mexican
DRINKS: Full Bar
SERVING: Lunch, Dinner
PRICE RANGE: $
NEIGHBORHOOD: Roma Norte
Chef Paloma Ortiz offers a menu featuring a variety of traditional recipes with a contemporary flair. There's a big emphasis on the *moles* from Oaxaca Sierre Norte region. Menu favorites include: Smoky chichilo and the classic tlayuda. Desserts include a multi-dimensional multi-layer chocolate cake made with Oaxacan chocolate. At night the place becomes a hip hangout.

Chapter 5
NIGHTLIFE

BALTRA
Iztaccíhuatl 36D, Cuauhtemoc, Mexico City, +52 55 5264 1279

www.baltra.bar

NEIGHBORHOOD: Condesa

Casual bar that offers a unique selection of cocktails – many created with tea leaves as one of the ingredients. Great selection of liquors.

Great comfortable bar with unique cocktails, knowledgeable bartenders and good design!

EL DEPÓSITO
Álvaro Obregón 21, Local 1, Mexico City, 52-55-5088-5552
www.eldeposito.com.mx
NEIGHBORHOOD: Condesa
This is part of a small chain of beer-bar-bottle shops that offer a wide selection of over 160 beers. Here you'll find a great selection of beer on tap, Mexican micros, European imports, German beers and a few Belgians. There's a terrace, TV, and free popcorn.

EL UNDER
Monterey 80, Col. Roma, 52 55 5511 5475
http://theunder.org/real/
NEIGHBORHOOD: Condesa
Another happening dance club.

FIFTY MILS
Paseo de la Reforma 500, Col. Juárez, México, D.F., +52 55 5230 1806

www.fiftymils.com
NEIGHBORHOOD: Juárez
Amazing quaint bar located in the **Four Seasons Hotel**. The Manhattan is their signature cocktail and it's top-notch. The bartenders are pros. But look closely at the "Creations" cocktail menu, which has cocktails unique to this wonderful lounge. Like Ant Man, which uses mescal, ants, egg whites, avocado, hoja santa bitters, soda water & lemongrass syrup. And that's just one cocktail! Plenty more to keep you busy. Hungry? Try the bar snacks like Grilled octopus with pineapple. Since you're here at the Four Seasons, try out the main restaurant, **IL BECCO**, featuring superior cuisine from the Piedmont region and a wondrous Italian wine list that will raise an eyebrow or two.

LA HERMOSA HORTENSIA
Callejón de la Amargura 4, Plaza Garibaldi 4, 52-55-5529-7828

No Website
NEIGHBORHOOD: Centro Norte
Located on the far corner of the Plaza Garibaldi, this
pulquería is a must-stop for visitors. It's a 77-year old
pulque bar that serves the lightly alcoholic Aztec
drink, made from the maguey plant. The drink has the
color of milk and comes in flavors like strawberry
and coconut. This bar is included in the Museos
Vivos project (which highlights "Living Museums"-
every day venues that have cultural and historic
significance).

LA NACIONAL
Orizaba 161, Mexico City, +52 55 5264 3106
No Website
NEIGHBORHOOD: Roma Norte
More of a bar than a restaurant with a very long list of
Mexican microbrews. Great local hangout.

LICORERIA LIMANTOUR
Alvaro Obregon 106, Mexico City, +52 55 5264 4122
www.limantour.tv
NEIGHBORHOOD: Roma Norte
Popular bar that has been awarded the title as being
"one of the best 50 bars in the world." Impressive
cocktail list. Menu of bar snacks available – fries
served with 4 different sauces.

M.N. ROY
Mérida 186, San Luis Potosi, 52 55 6681 0348
NEIGHBORHGOOD: Roma
www.mnroyclub.com
Emmanuel Picault opened this club and named it after
the Indian revolutionary and founder of the
Communist parties in both Mexico and India. It's
super cool and gorgeously designed. Had throbbing
house music late into the night. Dress to impress. It's
a slick crowd here, even though the outside is
designed to look like a simple ice cream parlor with a
door the color of pink carnations.

PATRICK MILLER

Mérida 17, Mexico City, 52 55 5511 5406
www.patrickmiller.com.mx
WEBSITE DOWN AT PRESSTIME
NEIGHBORHOOD: Roma Norte
This is an old school disco featuring high-energy '80s
dance music, laser lights and neon graffiti. Named
after a popular DJ, this club opened during the Gloria
Gayner golden days of disco and has been running
strong ever since. The eclectic crowd is filled with
flashy dressers, flamboyant transvestites, and disco
divas. No hard liquor here, just beer.

PULQUERIA LOS INSURGENTES

Ave. de los Insurgentes Sur 226, Mexico City, +52 55
5207 0917
No Website
NEIGHBORHOOD: Roma Norte
Typical dive bar with loud music and sawdust on the
floor. Multi-level bar including a dance floor. Menu

of bar snacks. Live music and DJs on weekends. They serve flavored pulque -blended fresh juice mixed with tequila.

TÍO PEPE
Av Independencia 26, 01 55 5521 9136
https://cantina-el-tio-pepe.negocio.site/
PRICE RANGE: $$
NEIGHBORHOOD: Centro Poniente
Located in Chinatown area, this old cantina is a locals' favorite. How they can stand the harsh florescent lights pulsating a nasty white light right above their heads is beyond me. It would be a lot nicer if they'd turn off those damn lights, or put in something nicer with a dimmer switch. Maybe light a candle? I should stop bitching, because I somehow always end up here one way or another. A nice ornately carved back bar touting Hennessy Cognac makes a stab providing some atmosphere. Simple menu of straight tequilas, brandies, rum and Cokes, and Fernets with soda. No food.

Chapter 6
WHAT TO SEE & DO

ANAHUACALLI MUSEUM
Museo 150, San Pablo Tepetlapa, Mexico City, +52
55 5617 3797
www.museoanahuacalli.org.mx
NEIGHBORHOOD: Coyoacán
Designed by Diego Rivera, this museum houses the
artist's quirky collection of over 60,000 pre-Hispanic
pieces. The museum is built out of black volcanic
stone and resembles a pyramid. The collection
includes funerary urns, masks, and sculptures from
the ancient culture of Teotihuacan. Minimal
admission fee.

ANTIGUO COLEGIO DE SAN ILDEFONSO

Justo Sierra 16, Mexico City, +52 55 3602 0035

www.sanildefonso.org.mx

NEIGHOBORHOOD: Centro Norte

This 18th-century former Jesuit school reopened as a museum and cultural center in 1992. The museum features permanent and temporary art and archeological exhibitions. Many come to view the many murals painted on the walls by artists like José Clemente Orozco, Fernando Leal, and Diego Rivera (who also has a lot of works on display at the **Palacio Nacional** a few blocks away). A gift shop is located in the patio of the Colegio Grande offering a selection of museum publications, handcrafted jewelry, ceramics and textiles.

CASA MUSEO LUIS BARRAGAN

General Francisco Ramirez 12, Mexico City, +52 55 5515 4908

www.casaluisbarragan.org

NEIGHBORHOOD: Daniel Garza

This is the former home of the great Mexican Modernist Luis Barragán. The museum is a must-see for lovers of architecture and exhibits Barragán's work. It's often used by visiting architects. Modest entrance fee.

CASTILLO DE CHAPULTEPEC

Bosque de Chapultepec, Mexico City, 52 55 4040 5215

https://mnh.inah.gob.mx/

NEIGHBORHOOD: Federal District
ADMISSION: Nominal fee, free on Sundays
Located on top of Chapultepec Hill, this is the only
Royal Castle in North America. It was used to house
the Mexican Emperor Maximilian I. This site was a

sacred place for Aztecs and the buildings were used
as a Military Academy, an Imperial residence, a
Presidential home and observatory. Today the hilltop
castle houses the **Museo Nacional de Historia
(National History Museum)**, with marble terraces,
fountains and historic artifacts. You can climb up on
foot (I did it one, but never again). It's worth the trip
for the views alone. But the fountains, the marble
floors and the historical exhibits make it even more
special. Manet made a famous painting Maximilian's
execution, and you can see how it was influenced by

Goya's painting "The Third of May 1808" depicting the execution of Spanish soldiers resisting Napoleon's invasion of Spain in the Peninsular War.

CENTRO CULTURAL UNIVERSITARIO
(University Cultural Center)
Avenida Insurgentes Sur 3000, Mexico City, 52 55 5622 7185
www.cultura.unam.mx
Located in a woodsy section of the university campus, this center is comprised of five theaters, including the Sala Nezahualcóyotl, home of the UNAM Philharmonic; the Teatro Alarcón, a drama stage; and the Sala Miguel Covarrubias, a contemporary dance venue. The cinema here shows Mexican and European films.

DAVID POMPA

Colima 264, Mexico City, +52 55 6583 5027

www.davidpompa.com

NEIGHBORHOOD: Roma Norte

Design studio of David Pompa selling high-end lighting and furniture. A favorite among designers.

EAT MEXICO CULINARY TOURS

Sinaloa 149, Mexico City, +52 1 55 3504 2135

www.eat-mexico.com

NEIGHBORHOOD: Roma

Small private culinary tours of Mexico City. Get a taste of what the locals eat. This tour takes you through the streets of Central Mexico where you'll sample street food, tacos and visit select markets. You'll also get a history of the food you're eating. Tours led by local, bilingual guides who share local history and culinary tips. Six routes to choose from. Tours are approximately 4 hours long.

ELENA GARRO CULTURAL CENTER

Calle Fernández Leal No. 43, Mexico City, +52 55 3003 4081

www.educal.com.mx/elenagarro/

NEIGHBORHOOD: Coyoacán,

Beautiful cultural center designed my Mexican architects Fernanda Canales and Arquitectura 911sc. An old house has been transformed into a modern looking cultural center with a library and series of gardens and courtyards.

GOODBYE FOLK

Colima 198, Cuauhtémoc, Mexico City, +52 55 5525 4109

www.goodbyefolk.com

NEIGHBORHOOD: Roma

Unique boutique that offers fashions and custom made shoes with an onsite hair salon.

Boutique. hairdresser, shoes made to order, free to all Mexico. Boutique, hair salon, custom made shoes. - we ship all around the world. Fashions like jackets, sweaters, and shirts all have a vintage feel.

HILARIO GALGUERA

Francisco Pimentel 3, Mexico City, 52 55 5546 9001

www.galeriahilariogalguera.com/nueva

NEIGHBORHOOD: San Rafael

Perfect place to catch up top-notch contemporary Mexican artists' work, like Bosco Sodi and Daniel Lezama. Also exhibits international artists like Damien Hirst.

JARDÍN BOTÁNICO (Park)

Av. Paseo de la Reforma S/N, Mexico City + 52 55 5286 6519

www.ibiologia.unam.mx/jardin/

ADMISSSION: Free

NEIGHBORHOOD: University City

This park and garden highlights Mexico's plant diversity. The park is divided into 4 sections that reflect the country's different climate zones. One of the highlights of the park is a greenhouse filled with rare orchids, but as you stroll through the trails, you'll encounter volcanic rocks and see examples of cactuses and succulents that are endangered species. Closed on Mondays.

JUMEX MUSEUM
MUSEO JUMEX
Miguel de Cervantes Saavedra 303, 52 55 5395 2618
NEIGHBORHOOD: Granada
www.fundacionjumex.org
David Chipperfield designed the Jumex, which focuses on contemporary artwork. Opened November 2013. When I first saw this collection, it was called the Coleccion Jumex and was on view in an old juice factory a bit out of town where it was Latin America's largest privately held art collection. Think Cy Twombly, Pedro Reynes, etc. The whole thing makes a much better impression in the Chipperfield building, needless to say.

KURIMANZUTTO GALLERY
Gob. Rafael Rebollar 94, Col. San Miguel
Chapultepec, 52-55-5256-2408
www.kurimanzutto.com/en/
Though this gallery is known for representing the top Mexican artists working today, it also has an impressive roster of international artists. Gabriel Orozco, Damian Ortega, Daniel Guzman and Dr Lakra all exhibit their work here, as well as Rirkrit Tiravanija and Jimmie Durham, just to name a few of the more prominent names.

MERCADO DE XOCHIMILCO
Nuevo Leon, Colonia Xochimilco
Farmer's Market OPEN DAILY

NEIGHBORHOOD: Xochimilco
This open-air Farmer's Market offers great shopping
opportunities for farm-fresh produce and other items
like the city's best barbacoa de borrego (slow-cooked
lamb). The market is also a unique dining option with
a variety of Mexican dishes including barbeque,
quesadillas, tacos, stew, and pambazos.

METROPOLITAN CATHEDRAL
Plaza de la Constitución, Mexico City, 52 55 5510
0440
http://catedralmetropolitanacdmx.org
NEIGHBORHOOD: Central Historic District
Opened in 1813, this is one of the oldest and largest
Roman Catholic cathedrals in the Americas. This
cathedral also acts as the seat of the Roman Catholic
Archdiocese of Mexico. You can go to the roof of this

cathedral where the view is spectacular as it overlooks what's left of the ruins (in the Templo Mayor) of the Aztec city that once existed here. (That city was called Tenochtitlán—try saying that fast 5 times.) There's a bar and restaurant up here called **El Mayor**, so you can get a cool drink after the long climb up.

MUSEO CASA DE LEON TROTSKY

Ave. Rio Churubusco 410, Mexico City, +52 55 5658 8732

www.museocasadeleontrotsky.blogspot.com

NEIGHBORHOOD: Coyoacán

ADMISSION: Moderate fee

The house where exiled Russian leader Leon Trotsky spent his final days has been transformed into a museum. Looking more like a fortress than a home complete with turrets for armed guards, this site is the final resting place for one of the most important figures of the Russian Revolution.

All information in Spanish only. English guides available for groups of five or more with reservations.

MUSEO CASA DEL RISCO

Plaza de San Jacinto 15, Mexico City, +52 55 5616 2711

www.museocasadelrisco.org.mx

NEIGHBORHOOD: San Ángel

ADMISSION: Free

Founded in 1958, this Cultural Center exhibits Mexican and European painting, sculpture, applied arts, textile works, and art objects purchased by politician Don Isidro Fabela. Revolving exhibitions along with the permanent collection, a library and a gift shop.

MUSEO DEL JUGUETE ANTIGUO MÉXICO
Dr. Olvera 15, Mexico City, 52 55 5558 2100
www.museodeljuguete.mx
NEIGHBORHOOD: Doctores
This multistory museum and art space built originally to house the collection of Roberto Shimizu. The collection mainly consists of mass-produced toys like Mexican action figures, German-made racecars, dolls heads, game pieces and lucha libre wrestlers. Roberto starting his collection in 1955 when he hoarded all his toys. His son now runs this collection of 45,000 items in a place next door to an auto-body shop just south of downtown.

MUSEO DIEGO RIVERA ANAHUACALLI

Calle Museo 150, Mexico City, +52 55 5617 4310
www.museoanahuacalli.org.mx/en/
ADMISSION: Moderate fee
HOURS:11 a.m. – 5:30 p.m. Wed-Sun
Designed by Diego Rivera himself, this impressive
museum made of volcanic stone houses his collection
of pre-Columbian art. The collection includes nearly
50,000 pre-Hispanic art pieces. The second floor
features an exhibition room devoted to the works of
Diego Rivera.

MUSEO FRANZ MAYER

Av. Hidalgo 45, Centro Histórico, Guerrero, +52 55
5518 2266
https://franzmayer.org.mx
NEIGHBORHOOD: Historic District
ADMISSION: Moderate fee; Tuesdays Free
Occupies the old hospice of the San Juan de Dios
order, this museum is home to Latin America's
largest collection of decorative arts. The museum also
sponsors workshops and temporary exhibitions. Café
located in central garden courtyard.

MUSEO NACIONAL DE ANTROPOLOGIA

Av Paseo de la Reforma y Calzada Gandhi S/N,
Mexico City, +52 55 5553 6266
www.mna.inah.gob.mx
NEIGHBORHOOD: Polanco
This national museum is the most visited museum in
Mexico. Here you'll find significant archaeological
and anthropological artifacts from pre-Columbian
Mexico. Standout pieces include: the Piedra del Sol
(the Aztec calendar stone) and the 16th-century Aztec

statue of Xochipilli. The museum features 23 rooms of exhibitions filled with pre-Columbian treasures. An eye-opening collection.

PALACIO NACIONAL
National Palace
Avenida Pino Suarez, Corregidora esquina
Guatemala, Zócalo, 52 55 3688 1255
www.hacienda.gob.mx/cultura/museo_virtual_pal_na
c/shcp_mv.htm
Of the 150 museums you can visit in Mexico City, this perhaps ought to be your first stop. This building was begun in 1693. The Viceroys of New Spain lived here until the Revolution. They have the whole history of the country's rich cultural diversity on display in the numerous exhibits here. There are huge murals by Diego Rivera depicting the history of the country dating from its pre-Columbian era down through the Mexican Revolution. There's a replica of the first Mexican Congress, Recinto Legislativo. They have English-speaking tour guides.

SOUMAYA MUSEUM
MUSEO SOUMAYA

Blvd. Miguel de Cervantes Saavedra 303, 52 55 1103 9800

www.soumaya.com.mx

NEIGHBORHOOD: Granada

Billionaire Carlos Slim (some years, he's richer than Microsoft's Bill Gates, other years he comes in second or third) put up the money for this great place, which recently moved into a $70 million building, which itself is worth the trip. The Soumaya has the largest collection of Rodin sculptures in Latin America (including more than 350 works by Rodin alone, but that's just part of the 65,000 items Slim donated to the museum, which is named after his late wife). It's better on a weekday if you can manage it because it's less crowded.

SPANISH CULTURAL CENTER

Pasaje Cultural Guatemala 18 — Donceles 97, 55 5521 1925

www.ccemx.org

This Spanish cultural center features art exhibitions, plays, and music events. (There's a permanent exhibit of pre-Columbian art and artifacts, as well as rotating exhibits.) On the weekend (Thurs-Sat) you can see live music (indie, electronic and rock bands) on the terrace of the bar-restaurant. In the 1990s, this old mansion was in ruins until the Spanish government saved it as a historic monument to the city. The center hosts workshops, seminars, children's activities, cultural events and exhibitions.

Chapter 7
SHOPPING & SERVICES

CARLA FERNANDEZ

Av. Álvaro Obregón 200, Mexico City, +52 55 5510 9624

www.carlafernandez.com

NEIGHBORHOOD: Polanco

Carla Fernandez, one of Mexico's top designers, offers her fashions in this boutique. She's known for creating Taller Flora, a demi couture line with a distinct geometric style, co-designed by and using Mexican artisans. Her Pret-a-porter line is also available here. Her fashions have been featured in all the major fashion publications.

CHIC BY ACCIDENT
Orizaba 28, Colonia Roma Norte, México, 52 55 8117 1140
http://chic-by-accident.com
NEIGHBORHOOD: Roma Norte
Designer Emmanuel Picault brings together an exciting and very personal collection of artifacts from different parts of Mexico—furniture, accessories, art pieces, gift items—that will give you a new sense of the richness of the cultural heritage of this country.

COLONIA ROMA
This is one of the older historic neighborhoods in Mexico City that's now packed with shops, boutiques, antique stores, bars and cafes offering a dizzying array of merchandise, art and food. The architectural style is a mix of Art Deco and

"Porfirian," a mishmash of styles from Europe fashionable when President Porfirio Díaz was in office. The main streets to focus on are Álvaro Obregón and Calle Colima.

DULCERIA DE CELAYA

5 de Mayo 39, Mexico City, +52 55 5521 1787
www.dulceriadecelaya.com
NEIGHBORHOOD: Cuauhtémoc
Founded in 1874 and located in an Art Nouveau gem, this is a mecca for lovers of sweets. Here you'll find treats like candied pineapple, guava, and other exotic fruits along with almond paste, candied walnut rolls, and cajeta. Many of these traditional sweets can't be found anywhere else locally.

FABRICA SOCIAL

Calle Isabel la Católica 30, Mexico City, +52 55 5512 0730

www.fabricasocial.org

NEIGHBORHOOD: Historic District

This organization promotes the work of female textile artisans through mobile workshops. This is a great way to bring cultural awareness to communities and sell the work.

GALERÍA DANIEL LIEBSOHN

Londres 161-49, Plaza del Ángel, 52 55 5525 2050

www.liebsohn.com.mx

NEIGHBORHOOD: Juárez

In Daniel's excellent gallery you'll find Mexican and European antiques mixed with Italian and American vintage furniture from the 20th century: you may see a 15th-century Flemish painting beside a lineal seat by Frank Kyle next to a 19th-century Napoleon III-style mirror. There's no other gallery like Daniel's in Mexico City. He has the best taste.

MERCADO DE MEDELLÍN (MARKET MEDELLIN)

Roma Sur, Cuauhtémoc, Mexico City
NEIGHBORHOOD: Distrito Federal
This is a popular Farmers' Market, located on the corner of Medellin and Campeche, offering a variety of fresh produce, spices, fresh juices, whole pigs' heads, meat, and other fresh food items. You'll also find plants, flowers and other items sold in flea market style. This place will give you an idea of the kind of cultural shopping tradition that is being decimated by the arrival of the "supermercados," supermarkets. Closed Sundays.

MERCADO DE JAMAICA

Guillermo Prieto 45, Jamaica, Mexico, +52 55 5741 0002
www.mercadodejamaica.com

NEIGHBORHOOD: Jardín Balbuena
This is a huge flower market that will have your head spinning.

MERCADO DE SAN JUAN
Calle Ernesto Pugibet número 21
www.mercadosanjuan.galeon.com
NEIGHBORHOOD: Centro Poniente
Chefs shop here for foods they later sell you in their restaurants. It's really a unique place where you can get exotic meats like crocodile, ostrich, lion, deer and exotic fruits and vegetables, sweets, spices, meats, cheeses and products it's impossible to find anywhere else. In all probability, you're not there to buy meats and cheeses, but like me, you just want to mix with the local crowds. This is a scene unlike any other. (Great place to buy gift items.) Watch out for pickpockets.

MUSEO TAMAYO
Paseo de la Reforma 51, Mexico City, 52 55 4122 8200
www.museotamayo.org/
NEIGHBORHOOD: Morelos
Not only a great museum but also a great place to purchase art, it's near the National Museum of Anthropology in Chapultepec Park. This museum, run by the Tamayo Foundation, is primarily dedicated to the collection of artist Rufino Tamayo and other contemporary artists like Sophie Calle and Yayoi Kusama.

PANADERÍA ROSETTA (Bakery)
Colima 166, Colonia Roma, Mexico City, 52 55 5207 2976
www.rosetta.com.mx/
NEIGHBORHOOD: Roma Norte
This small bakery offers a variety of classic Mexican baked goods like pan de pulque conchas as well as delicious croissants, and vegan muffins. The menu also includes well-made espresso drinks, sandwiches and house-made pâté.

SANGRE DE MI SANGRE
Orizaba 101, Mexico City, 52 55 5511 8599
www.sdemis.com
NEIGHBORHOOD: Roma Norte
Located in a bohemian neighborhood, this is a celebration of art and beauty through Sangre de mi Sangre's jewelry designed by Mariana Villarreal. She has two lines and her jewelry has been featured in Vogue, Harper's Bazaar, and Elle magazines.

THE SHOPS AT DOWNTOWN
Isabel La Católica 30, Mexico City
www.theshops.mx
NEIGHBORHOOD: Historic Center
Located in the courtyard of the stately colonial home
of the Counts of Miravalle, built originally in 1846, is
a collection of over 20 unique shops offering food,
crafts, culture and design. The building was saved in
1985 and converted into a commer   cial enterprise.

INDEX

DID YOU FIND AN INTERESTING PLACE?
If you discover a place you think I should check out
on my next visit, drop me a line, will you? I'll
mention your name if I end up listing it.
andrewdelaplaine@mac.com

WANT 3 FREE THRILLERS?

Why, of course you do!

If you like these writers--
Vince Flynn, Brad Thor, Tom Clancy, James
Patterson, David Baldacci, John Grisham, Brad
Meltzer, Daniel Silva, Don DeLillo

If you like these TV series – Madam Secretary, Designated Survivor, House of Cards, Scandal, West Wing, The Good Wife,

You'll love the **unputdownable** series about Jack Houston St. Clair, with political intrigue, romance, and loads of action and suspense.

Besides writing travel books, I've written political thrillers for many years that have delighted hundreds of thousands of readers. I want to introduce you to my work!
Send me an email and I'll send you a link where you can download the first 3 books in my bestselling series, absolutely FREE.

Mention **this book** when you email me.

andrewdelaplaine@mac.com

CPSIA information can be obtained
at www.ICGtesting.com
Printed in the USA
LVHW010208280120
645026LV00002B/457